Pops, how come Everton won the League in '87?

John D. Fowler

Author's Acknowledgement

The poem 'Playing the Blues', and the lines on the front cover, are written by John Fagan, a brilliant local author and poet who has had a number of books published by Countyvise Ltd.
Thanks also to Kenny Hatton for designing the front and back cover.

Every effort has been made to fulfil requirements with regard to reproducing copyright material. The author and publisher will be glad to rectify any omissions.

First Published 2010 by Countyvise Ltd
14 Appin Road, Birkenhead, CH41 9HH

Copyright © 2010 John D. Fowler

British Library Cataloguing in Publication Data.
A catalogue record for this book is available from the British Library.

ISBN 978 1 906823 43 6

DEDICATION

This book is dedicated to my grandsons, Jamie and Robbie Gibson,
also with mention to my son Paul and daughter
Jennie and her husband Ben.
'Great Evertonians' - well brought up.

My other daughter, Naomi, and my wife, Paula, lean
towards the other side. Every family has black sheep.

PREFACE

"POPS, HOW DID EVERTON WIN THE TITLE?"

My Dad first took me to Goodison Park early in the 1950s, probably when I was about 8 years old. I do not remember who Everton were playing that day, but we were in the Second Division at the time.

At that age I did not understand the situation, and we could have been playing on Mars as far as I was concerned, I just loved the atmosphere, and was hooked from that day on.

Apart from collecting programmes, I started the hobby of making scrapbooks. Some of any sport, some of Liverpool Football Club, but mainly of my beloved Everton.

I would studiously cut out reports and pictures from newspapers and magazines, and stick them in my cheap scrapbooks, which were instantly transformed into a rich world of fantasy and dreams. The times I scored the winning goal in the Gladwys St. End were innumerable.

Fast forward into the Eighties, I am taking my son (age 12), and youngest daughter (age 8) to watch a match, from the Family Club, together with my mates and their young children. We are witnessing Everton's finest period. My eldest daughter and her mother have had to be sectioned as they are supporting the boys in red, but it made for some exciting moments in our house.

For some unexplained reason, at the start of the 1986/87 season, I reverted back to my childhood (no I did not start wearing short trousers, but I still enjoyed a feisty game of Ollies), and decided to make a scrapbook. I began to cut out the reports and religiously (yes, I think I did it every Sunday) STUCK to my routine. The scrapbook became a detailed report on the season, but little did I know we would win the league that year.

So it has now become a rare individual record and probably worth a fortune on the Antiques Roadshow - if only! I'd probably get more for my wife, except she is not stamped on the bottom. She wasn't the last time I sneaked a look, following a drunken night-out in 1968 - well it was the "Swinging Sixties" - which is what we now are...

I have two grandsons now, who, when they can draw themselves away from their I-pods, MP3s, or whatever they are called (I have got a Bluetooth, but that's part of supporting the Toffees - and eating them), are interested in football in general, but they cannot decide who to support yet on a permanent basis. It will be the next team that wins something. Long time to wait then.

When I discovered my old scrapbooks, my youngest grandson was particularly intrigued as to how a small time club, with no money could possibly win the league.

How the heck did we do it?

Since the Premier League, and indeed The Champions League, were formed, it has developed into a vicious circle, with only 3 or 4 clubs, with the money to buy the world's top players, having a chance of winning the title. All the other clubs, including Everton, can only strive for a place in the Europa league. No wonder some people are now calling it boring, a bit like the Scottish Premier League, where only two clubs contest it.

If things continue in this vein, 1986/87 was probably the last time Everton will ever win the title - and as some Welsh rugby fanatic (Max Boyce) used to say, "I WAS THERE".

This brilliant book (possibly a film could be made of it, if they can get Robert Redford to play my part) is an account of a grandfather going through the scrapbook, outlining the reports, and explaining to his grandson how we did it.

Playing the Blues

We were checking the football scores one Saturday night,
After another disaster against the Arsenal might.
How long is it Granddad since we last won the league,
His reaction was imminent, he was a man of intrigue.
Granddad, looked up and scratched his bald head,
I knew by his eyes, we'd be late going to bed.

'I'll gather my wits lad' he replied, deep in thought,
And smiled to himself at the battles well fought
It was back in the eighties, twenty three years ago,
He was brimming with pleasure his face now aglow.
Four brilliant years were etched deep in his heart,
Winning the F.A Cup, that's where he would start.

Eighty four was the date, son, he remembered quite well,
Andy Gray smacked the winner like a bat out of hell.
We then graced our talent the following year,
Against Rapid Vienna, which we won without fear.
In Rotterdam City the final was played,
After conquering Europe reputations were made.
Eighty seven arrived, what a glorious team,
Winning the league again, now that was my dream.

He was full of arthritis after years on the docks,
His medicine was typical, 'a scotch on the rocks.'
Give me a minute son, while I go for a pee,'
I noticed him wobbling on his dodgy left knee.
Sneaking a blimp at his counterfeit watch,
"Whereabouts where we up to", he swallowed his scotch.

I'll now test me marbles, try an` remember a few names.
Big Nev was our goalie from Llandudno North Wales.
There was Sharpie and Sheedy and Adrian Heath.

A strike force well known for baring their teeth.
Now Sheedy was gifted with a perfect left foot,
A ball on a sixpence he could place without fuss.

Trevor Steven was stylish, Kevin Ratcliffe a star,
Paul Power well named, Allan Harper on par.
Dave Watson a hero Derek Mountfield was cool,
Bobby Mimms and Neil Pointon were nobody's fools.
But stealing the thunder was a manager of merit,
And Howard deserved all the praise and the credit.

John Fagan

INTRODUCTION

With big money now the dominant force in English football, the Premier League title is won by the richest clubs. It has now got to the point where the experts feel only the four richest clubs have a chance of winning it. Ironically, Liverpool are included in the so-called 'big four', but the last title they won was in 1990. Bearing in mind, that it is now generally known, Everton are a relatively poor club, the logic is they will never win the League again. So what happened in 1986/87? How did we win it? Youngsters who support the club must wonder what it was like to have a team who finished the season as the best in the land. To finish 5th now is counted as a major achievement but years ago it was a failure.

1986 arrived and since 1984 Howard Kendall had built Everton into one of the top teams in the country and along with their Merseyside rivals, Liverpool, they were sharing the major prizes. This was a period of great success in our history, and after years in the doldrums the supporters could hold their heads high and there was great friendly banter in the city.

At the end of the previous season, we left the illustrious Double (F.A. Cup and League) to, of all people, our deadly rivals Liverpool. No matter what the records say, all good Evertonians thought 'we wuz robbed'.

Going into the new season we were confident as we still had great players and a great manager. We feared no-one - only the wife.

The pre-season build-up contained the usual surprises, but unlike now the big money was abroad, and so our game lost Mark Hughes and our own Gary Lineker to Barcelona, whose manager was Terry Venables. It was inevitable he would sign top British players.

1986 Charity Shield at Wembley - Everton and Liverpool fans together.
Above - Author with his son Paul.
Below - Author.

To everybody's surprise, Liverpool's goalscoring hero, Ian Rush, signed an agreement to join Juventus, but was to remain at Anfield for one more season.

Most of the big transfers between English clubs were around the £700,000 mark. The Blues spent £900,000 on signing Dave Watson from Norwich.

It was a surprise for Everton fans, who were not particularly overwhelmed at the time.

The official season kicked off with the Charity Shield against the 'auld enemy' Liverpool at the old Wembley stadium. Both sets of supporters were beginning to get a bit blasé about this type of fixture and treated it as 'our day out'. The weather was a typical sunny August day, the supporters were relaxed and friendly, and most coaches contained equal numbers of Reds and Blues. Despite the fact there was a capacity crowd of 88,000, the 1-1 draw was dull and lacklustre, and the fans came away feeling the result had been 'choreographed', for want of a better word.

Liverpool had been very successful in the 70s and Everton, at last, produced a team who looked like maintaining lasting success. Merseyside was dominating English football in the mid-eighties, at a time when foreign players were few and far between, as most of the world stars migrated to Italy or Spain.

This was a time before Sky TV began pouring money into the game. Clubs did not have billionaire sugar daddies, but it was still the nation's favourite sport. Chelsea were very ordinary and Man.Utd were struggling in the lower half of the table.

The Premier League had not been invented, and the First Division was it's equivalent. The league was sponsored by the now defunct tabloid newspaper 'Today'. It was famous for being the first newspaper to print colour photos. Not only is it now defunct, it is no longer in existence. There was a joke going round that clubs announced "yesterday, tomorrow's team for the Today game." The scene was set - let proceedings begin.

As a footnote it was reported that one of the Everton directors was on his way to Wembley in his Rolls Royce, when his chauffeur lost his way. Stopping, he leant out of the window and asked a fan. "Is this the best way to Wembley?" "Well, it's a damn sight better than walking" came the reply.

AUGUST

"Pops, did you keep a scrapbook for every season?"

I used to make one every season whilst I was a youngster. It is so easy to make, you just cut out of the papers or magazines any stories or reports about your favourite team, and stick them in your book. My mother used to make me paste out of flour and water, so if she had a row with Dad, I would STICK up for her.

"Pops, your jokes are getting worse. Why did you start a scrapbook for 1986/87 season? You were a grown up kid by then."

I don't know. I must have had a premonition that we would win the League for the last time, because it is something you cannot start in retrospect. The thing about a scrapbook is that it brings back the memories and makes them more vivid .

"Will you tell me the story of the season, Pops? I am dying to hear it. How did Everton win the league? We have got no chance now, unless a multi-Billionaire buys us".

I have got innumerable memories so I will try to recall them as best as I can, but don't forget it was the last century...

One of the most wonderful moments in soccer, if not the most magical, is the first game of a new season. The expectation, the anticipation, the build-up in the press and on TV. Is this going to be your team's year? In those days there were no large televised pre-season tournaments or friendlies. They were more low key and this added to the mystery. There was no summer transfer window. Everything seemed fresh, and whether it's true, the sun always seemed to shine.

The stadium had usually been painted and spruced up, the grass was greener, and the pitch was perfect. The players had been honing their limbs to perfection, and the sun tans from their summer exploits made them look fitter. Supporters had washed their scarves and underpants, and oiled their rattles.

"What's a rattle, Pops? Is it like Nana`s teeth?"

Yes, but not as noisy. Well, in the real old days, supporters would have this heavy wooden contraption which you spun around with your hand and it made a rat-tat-tat sound. So you can imagine the noise it made when thousands had them.

"Did you have one?"

Yes, when I was a kid, but by 1986 I think they had been banned because they could have been used as a dangerous weapon. It was a sign of how football had changed from the 40s and 50s, through the hooligan years of the 70s.

Anyway, back to the first game. The biggest problem we had was a horrific injury list, plus, the disappointment of last season's ending, losing the double. Also, many of our players had taken part in the World Cup, so they were bound to be tired. We had also sold our star player, Gary Lineker.

"What happened with Gary Lineker? I was made up telling my school friends he played for us."

Well, we won the league in 1985, and as Andy Gray was at the veteran stage, they decided to let him go and signed Lineker, who had been a prolific scorer at his home town club, Leicester City. Andy had been marvellous at Everton, and I personally would have liked to have seen him play with Gary, but it was not to be.

Lineker was the young up and coming star of English football, and we all thought this would be the icing on the cake and we would be invincible. Unfortunately we did not win anything.

"Was it his fault?"

Oh no, he was a brilliant, fast player and a great goal scorer. We tended to play a different game using the long ball a bit more.

Nothing wrong with that. I had seen us under the cosh many times, when suddenly a through ball would fly over the top of their back four, and Gary would sprint away and we would be 1-0 up. You always felt that with him in the team we would score. He was a gentleman on the field, never booked. A nice guy - I remember when he first signed, they had a 'Family' day at Bellefield, where the fans could meet the players and see them train. Gary (as did all the players) signed autographs and chatted to the fans in pouring rain. He always seemed to have a smile on his face.

"Why didn't we win anything?"

I think it was just a bit of bad luck. We were runners-up, by the skin of our teeth. But even if we had won the double, Gary would have moved on.

He had been the England star in the World Cup and Barcelona, with Terry Venables, came to call, and not forgetting English clubs were banned from the European competition, so all round it was an offer for club and player that could not be refused.

It was a great shame. I would have loved to have kept him for one more year, but I was proud he had worn the Blue of Everton. But, remember, Sunbeam, once anybody leaves Everton, they are on the way down.

Anyway, looking at our fixture list, the first 6 games were against such high and mighty names as Notts Forest, Sheffield Wed, Coventry, Oxford Utd, QPR and Wimbledon. You will laugh at these names now but back in the eighties they had strong teams. These days it is the clubs with the riches that prevail but back then anybody thought they had a chance.

Goodison Park in the 1980s - "Notice the old Park End stand. Who says there is a post in the way?"

Our first game was home to Notts Forest, who were managed by one of the most famous managers in the game, Brian Clough, whose teams always played good football. Cloughie, who called himself 'Old Big 'Ed,' had a mouth as big as the Mersey Tunnel, and like that famous landmark, it took its toll. He was never afraid to speak his mind and often caused controversy, and this probably cost him the England job. Generally the fans liked him, and he created interest and got everybody talking.

He had a great track record, and was responsible for paying the first £1 million transfer for Trevor Francis, but it soon paid off as he scored the winning goal to secure the European Cup. Imagine little Old Notts Forest doing that today. Even John Lennon couldn't imagine that.

What I liked about Cloughie was that when he was a centre forward for Middlesborough in the 2nd Division, he was a prolific goal scorer, and you know what, he always seemed to bag a few against Liverpool. Forest were a strong side, with players like Stuart Pearce, who became renowned for wearing his heart on his sleeve; and his own son, Nigel. They had also signed a Dutch international named Johnny Metgod from Real Madrid, which was unusual in those days.

Despite having seven players missing through injury, we won 2-0, which really highlighted the squad strength and management skills. Both goals came from the trusted left peg of Kevin Sheedy, operating on the left side of mid-field in a 4-4-2 system.

Sheeds was signed from Liverpool reserves a few seasons earlier, and having been given a decent run in the team, he soon became a first pick and a crowd pleaser, because basically he was a class act. His left foot was commonly known in the trade as "educated", and probably would have qualified for an honours degree, whereas his right foot would have been sought after by the truancy officers. His greatest strength was his passing ability, and his dead-ball free kicks. He was that good that when we got a free-kick just outside the box it was almost as good as a penalty, he was that accurate.

It was probably better than a penalty to witness, because of the usual long setting up of a defensive wall, with the crowd chanting "Sheedee, Sheedee". It became such a ritual, that sometimes even when he was not playing, they still chanted his name. The build-up, and the anticipation, and the end result of the ball nestling in the top corner of the net was a memory to behold. He once planted a beauty in the top corner, against Ipswich in a cup game, only to be ordered to re-take it for some infringement. We all thought he could not do it again because obviously the goalkeeper and defence would now suss him out. He then calmly put the next kick in the opposite corner of the net, like a star golfer chipping a ball to a precise spot. The crowd went crazy.

Anyway back to the game, the attendance was 35,000, which was good considering most of the Stanley Park end was closed, awaiting to be knocked down and rebuilt. I think it had been condemned by the Council, like my jokes.

Most Blues fans would have settled for the result before the game, given our weakened team, and playing against one of our closest rivals.

By the way, Sunbeam, Gary Lineker scored both Barcelona goals on his league debut. I felt dead jealous.

Two days later we had a tough away fixture at Sheffield Wednesday, who never forgave us for our magnificent comeback in the 1966 F.A. Cup final.

"How did a team get such a name as Wednesday, Pops?"

Well they were originally formed from a cricket team, who could only play on half-day closing day, which happened to be a Wednesday. All the shops used to close on Wednesday afternoon in those days, I think it was the law. Just think if it had been another day, they might have been called Sheffield Monday.

"Were Blackburn Rovers named after a dog?"

Just don't ask about Arsenal!!

I personally never liked playing Wednesday, as they always seemed to be a gritty, workmanlike lot, and you knew it was always going to be a physical battle. Typical down-to earth Yorkshire grit.

"Did you say grit, Pops?"

Hey, there was a famous old story from way back. Wednesday were going through a bad spell, and the manager kept going on about the team lacking bite. The left winger, apparently was a bit of a joker, and he kept telling the lads he would arrange it, and so one day he produced a ferret from his pocket. The dressing room soon cleared.

"I will bet he had a flat cap on"

Who, the player or the ferret?

Anyway, back to the game. We had to show tremendous fighting qualities to come back not just once, but twice. It was reported that both front men, Sharp and Heath, battled away tirelessly, with Sharp scoring an outstanding goal. The "Man of the match" award went to young Kevin Langley, who got the equaliser in the 2-2 draw.

Langley was signed from 3rd Division Wigan, and at 6ft tall, he looked a good prospect and somebody who could eventually replace the great Peter Reid, who was one of the walking wounded. Such was our injury crisis, young reserve striker Paul Wilkinson played in midfield.
Other players on the long term injury list were Neville Southall, Pat Van Den Hauwe, Gary Stevens, Derek Mountfield, Paul Bracewell, and Neil Pointon.

These were all proven top class players, who had been regulars in the previous successful teams, so you could see what a difficult job Howard Kendall had on his hands.

Derek Mountfield was the first player expected to be fit, but he faced a tough battle to regain his place at centre back, as we had signed Dave Watson from Norwich for a record fee. Dave was a tough customer, what you would call a "stopper". Mountfield was a popular player; very quick with a lot of skill. He could also score goals from set pieces, but he had been out for a long time so the fans were wondering where he would fit in. When someone is out for a long time with a bad injury you always wonder whether they will come back the same.

Mid-fielder, Kevin Richardson, who had been a squad player for the past few years, was looking for first team action, so he decided to move to Watford, managed by a future England manager, Graham Taylor. Kevin was a hard grafter who always did a good job without becoming a regular, so no one could blame him for leaving. He went on to forge a fine career, particularly later on with Arsenal.

The last game of the beautiful month of August, when my birthday passed by without a murmur, was away to Coventry City.

"Who?"

I know, I know, but they were "dead good" in those days, or shall we say of a similar standard to Sheffield Wed. More teams then were on a level playing field, money wise.

Coventry had risen from nowhere to First Division status, that is today's equivalent of the Premier League. Much of the credit for the rise appeared to be down to Jimmy Hill, plus obviously a great number of unknowns behind the scene. Over the years Jimmy seemed to have done everything at Coventry, and I mean everything, probably including the washing of the kit.

He seemed to be responsible for getting players better wages, and his enthusiasm and knowledge of the game was infectious.
"I had a sty on my eye once and the doctor said it was infectious."

19

Same thing son, he was always in your face on TV. I remember seeing him playing for Fulham at Goodison, and he was a very hardworking inside forward, you know, in midfield. He was once described in the notes of an Everton programme as "one of the few players who sported a beard". Other players got vivid descriptions of their ability, but I suppose he became just as famous for his beard over a large protruding chin as he did for his football brain. Very similar to Brucie Forsyth, but not as nimble on his feet.

The game was a dull 1-1 draw, but at least we were still unbeaten. A young lad named Neil Adams made his debut on the wing and did quite well. He was small and tricky, but he had a hard act to follow in Trevor Steven, who switched to midfield and was our best player. It was a 20 year old sub, Ian Marshall, who got our equaliser. He was a big lad who looked promising.

"Did he only use one sub?"

Well you were only allowed one then. Nowadays you need a little stand to accommodate them all.

So the first month of the season was over, and although we had not set the world alight, at least we were unbeaten. One win and two away draws.

God was in his heaven, or in this case, Diego Maradona, who was considered the world's best player, and was proving it by turning small-time Napoli into champions of Italy. Maggie Thatcher, the Iron lady, was ruling the land, but us Evertonians were optimistic, because we had lots of great players to return to our team and they would be like new signings, so we hoped to have a good season.

"I notice from the photos in the scrapbooks, Pops, that moustaches were in fashion".

Aye, and that was just the women.

NORTH TERRACE SEATS
(Uncovered)

ENTER AT TURNSTILES
(See Plan on back)

ENTRANCE

D 1

Row **12** Seat **15**

EMPIRE STADIUM, WEMBLEY

The Football Association Cup Competition

FINAL TIE

SATURDAY, APRIL 29th, 1933
(Kick-off 3 p.m.)

Price 5/–
(Including Tax)

A. J. Elvin

MANAGING DIRECTOR,
Wembley Stadium Limited.

THIS PORTION TO BE RETAINED
(See Conditions on back)

"It was my Dad's fault that my love affair with Everton started. Taking me to games when I was very young and telling me stories about Dixie...
"This is his ticket stub for the F.A. Cup final in 1933, when we beat Manchester City 3-0. This final was historic in that they were the first teams to have numbers on their shirts (how does five European cups compare with that?)."

"How did you get into following Everton?"

Well, like everybody else, it was my dad, your great Grandad, that took me. He used to leave me in the Boy's Pen, and I was 27 at the time, then he would take up his favourite spot near the church at the Gladys Street end. We would meet after the game and he had usually lost his voice from shouting, and he was normally so quiet.

"That was good of him, taking everybody else."

You know what I mean, fathers pass on their fanaticism to their sons.

"I thought Uncle Jim was a Liverpudlian?"

Yeah, my brother, and when my dad found out, he wanted to have him adopted, but my Mum stuck up for the Reds, so it was a mixed marriage.

All I ever got from Dad were tales of Albert Geldard, Cliff Britton, Jackie Coulter, and Alec Stevenson, but most of all Dixie Dean. The way he talked of him, he must have been some player - he said they used to just swing the ball across and Dean would leap and head it into the net. His record of 60 goals in one season certainly proved the stories true. He said he saw him score with a header once from outside the box. Dean was a legend, but the tales of his exploits became a legend as well, and as with most old anecdotes, they became exaggerated with the repetitive story telling. According to Dad, Dixie used to get the tram to the game, with the rest of the supporters, have 19 pints of bitter in the Wilmslow, go and get changed ten minutes before the match, and score with a header from the half-way line - and that was from the kick-off.

"Did you believe him, Pops?"

Nah, I think 19 was too much.

"Who was your favourite player when you first went?"

It was back in the early Fifties, and I loved an inside forward called Wally Fielding, known as Nobby.

"Why was he called Nobby?"

Because all small lads were given the nickname Nobby in those days.

"Why wasn't one of the seven dwarfs called Nobby then?"

I think Dopey was known as Nobby to his mates down at the pub.

"Why?"

Because he was nuts.

Anyway, Fielding was a ball-player, a dribbler, who could also split defences with great passes. He used to wear his long sleeves over his hands, and was a crowd pleaser, a cheekie-chappy type of man who stood out from the rest. Also at that time, we had Dashing Davie Hickson at centre-forward, the opposite to Nobby. He did not possess his skill, but was a passionate player who gave the fans 100% effort, and with his shock of blond hair, he always attracted attention. In those days most teams had big robust centre halves, who liked to impose themselves on the opposition, but Davie used to give as good as he got, and at most matches the crowd witnessed a battle and loved Davie getting stuck-in to the bullies. He also scored some spectacular goals, particularly with his head. An Everton legend.

Some years later, when I left school, I joined New Brighton F.C. who were a leading Non-League side at the time, and their player-manager was a chap named Cyril Lello, who had played left-half for the Blues during the 50s. Having been a first team regular, he was naturally one of my boyhood heroes, so you can imagine how I felt playing in the same team as him at 18 years of age. Lello was at the veteran stage then, but I learnt more about football from him in a short space of time than I had learned from playing schoolboy football up to that point.

"What sort of things, Pops?"

He taught me about movement off the ball, anticipation, positional sense, planning the next pass before the ball comes to you, but mainly about "shouting" and talking constantly to team-mates.

"If you had all this knowledge, how come you never made it as a professional?"

Well, you also needed determination, fitness, speed, stamina, skill, and a lorra', lorra' luck. I always said that if Alf Ramsay had seen me play, I would have been in the World Cup team of 1966. But, unfortunately, he never came to our park.

"Who else did you like?"

I will tell you later.

SEPTEMBER

"Pops, how come we were playing a non-league team in the next game?"

You may well think that, but many moons ago, in the dark ages, Oxford were not a non-league team, you will be surprised to learn. Every now and again by a simple twist of fate, usually aided by a multi-millionaire's dosh, a minnow or small-town club would rise, totally unexpectedly, and even without warning, to the top division in the country. Such a team were from the university town of Oxford, adding a United to their name.

"I'll bet they were dead clever. Did they have Latin numbers on their backs?"

Well "studying" form, and having done my "homework", I had the game down as a home banker.

On a wet Saturday afternoon, The Blues duly obliged with a 3-1 win, but it was not easy at first. It was obvious they had been working out a system on the blackboard and they succeeded to some degree, but it was us that got the honours. I hope you got all those little puns, Sunbeam!

"Don't give up your day job, Pops!"

They had come with a defensive sweeper system, which we found hard to break down for 50 minutes. Then Inchy Heath was brought down in the penalty area by their keeper, and despite vigorous protests that he had dived, the penalty was slotted home by Trevor Steven.

"I suppose the goalie would have been sent off in today's environment"

You are right, but he wasn't.

"Did they have diving in those days?"

Now, come on. Would a nice little blue-eyed Evertonian dive? No way. Oxford equalised shortly afterwards, but goals from Alan Harper and Kevin Langley secured the points. Included in Oxford's team were future Anfield favourites, Ray Houghton and John Aldridge, so you can see how crap they were.

"Who was Alan Harper?"

He was signed from Liverpool Reserves in 1982, and under our brilliant coaching, he became probably the best utility player in the game at the time. Although he was primarily a right back, he was called on to play any defensive position, and he never let us down. He was one of those unfortunate players who was a "jack of all trades", so he never became a regular in any position. It was reported he was on the same money as when he signed, but at this stage he was on a weekly contract and no club had made an offer for him. His main concern was that his favourite position, right back, was taken by the current England international, Gary Stevens. Eventually he signed a new contract, which I presume was on better money.

At this stage Everton were supposed to be seeing the light at the end of the tunnel on the injury front. England midfielders Peter Reid and Paul Bracewell were having their plasters removed. They must have been on their fingers as it was a long time before they played.

Our next home game against Queens Park Rangers was described as a dour 0-0 draw, and we looked short on class, which was hardly surprising given our long term injury list. Only thing to note from the game was the opposition where a certain David Seaman was in goal - if only the Blues knew that his weakness was 30 yard lobs. Another recent signing for them was little Sammy Lee from Liverpool - I once saw Sammy Lee and Kenny Dalglish walking towards me by

Other views of the beloved Goodison Park.

the Adelphi Hotel, and in true 'Scouse' style, Sammy "codded on" to me, so I will never have a word said against him. I am sure I heard Dalglish say to him, "How the hell do you know John Fowler?"

Sunbeam, have you ever heard who was the best goalie ever? I will give you a clue, he was famous for making a great save from Pele in the World Cup.

"Was it Gordon Banks?"

Correct. Well, we signed him.

"You must be joking, he must have had a grey beard by then."

It was reported that we had signed the greatest goalkeeper in the world to specialise in providing coaching to Bobby Mimms, Fred Barber, and Neville Southall. Banks, who was a World Cup hero in 1966, had his career ended in tragic circumstances in 1972, when a car crash cost him his right eye. Some wag in the crowd said he was brought in to keep an eye on our goalies, and to see if they were good pupils.

It was not a common practise in those days to have specialised coaches for one position, like it is now. It probably only lasted a week because we never heard anything about it afterwards. I do not think it was a permanent job, and anyway we had the best goalie in the world in Neville, although he was injured at the time.

Wimbledon, who were the self-styled "Crazy Gang" named after a popular London stage comic group, were our next opponents. The trouble with these geezers was it was only themselves and their fans who considered them to be remotely bordering on the amusing or entertaining. They had come from non-league football and risen to the First Division in rapid time, but their gung-ho, up and at 'em style won few admirers and likened them to a pub team playing in the Sunday League, which was an insult to the Liverpool Sunday league, which contained much better footballers.

It is not true that season ticket holders used to send in a doctor's note feigning a "Billiards" attack, when they came to town.

However, any game against "Wombledon" was considered difficult, and nobody enjoyed playing against them, especially at their small home stadium, which I think has now been knocked down.

Up to this point they were top of the League, but a magnificent header by Graeme Sharp added to Kevin Sheedy's opener, which sealed the points. Derek Mountfield played his first game of the season.

Graeme Sharp was a 6ft 1" Centre Forward, signed from Dumbarton some years earlier. He had scored 77 goals in 177 matches before the start of the season, and every newspaper report usually contained the following descriptions of Sharp's play: " a superb header", "battled tirelessly", "all round determination". "showed a great will-to-win" - always a 100 percenter. A perfect no.9 in the Everton tradition.

After 6 games, Notts Forest were top, Liverpool 2nd, we were 3rd and Wimbledon 4th. Newcastle were bottom.

Next match up was the beloved (and I don't think) Red Devils of Manchester Utd at Goodison. If there was one team we loved to beat, apart from the `Pool, it was our Mancunian friends, and in those days they were no problem as we always seemed to have the "glad eye" on them. They had some very good players but never seemed to produce consistency. Their star was Bryan Robson in midfield, nicknamed "Captain Marvel", because of his never-say-die attitude and driving displays. He was also England's best player at the time. They also had the likes of Gordon Strachan, who was a tricky, hardworking winger, Norman Whiteside, a very strong bullish striker, and Frank Stapleton, a skilful and experienced target man.

You would think with the players they had they would be at the top, but they just could not put it together on a regular basis, and we always looked forward to playing them.

At this game there was a relatively small crowd.

"What, no one over 6 ft?"

There was always one over 6ft in front of me. Only 25,000 turned up, and this was probably because it was live on TV - a bit of a novelty in those days. Anyway it was reported that millions of viewers saw United outfought by an Everton side ravaged by injury.

One of the consequences of the game was that flamboyant Ron Atkinson ("Big Ron") was having a bad time and the knives were out for him. The papers said that Graeme Sharp led the burial detail and put more nails in the United manager's coffin. The United players rallied round and stated "We play good football and soon the results will come." All the usual clichés. They would have been better pawning Big Ron's jewellery and buying a new attack.

Everton scorers were Sharp, Sheedy, and Heath popping one in a minute from time. Robson had actually equalised, but it was not an entertaining game, a non-event really.

However, it did prove a turning point in the history of Man U, and I suppose football in general, as shortly afterwards Atkinson was replaced by Alex Ferguson from Aberdeen. After a barren first five years, it has probably been the biggest success story in football, but something us Blues don't want to talk or even whisper about.

There was a joke doing the rounds, about an Evertonian who had died and God was taking him on a tour of heaven.

"Well", said God, "over there are Liverpudlians, City, Spurs, and Leeds supporters."
"What's that brick wall over there?" asked the Bluenose.
"The Man.Utd supporters are behind that, they think they are the only ones here."

In midweek we played in what is now called The Carling Cup. At that time it was the Littlewoods Cup, played over 2 legs. We were at home in the first leg to lowly Newport County, then members of the league, and we strolled it 4-0. Only 11,000 fans bothered to support the team, which showed you what they thought of this cup. The second leg was played two weeks later, and we won 5-1.

Our first league defeat came on 27th September against Spurs at White Hart Lane, so not a bad record considering all our injuries. Tottenham had always been associated with playing attractive football, ever since the days when they won the League and Cup double in 1961. They seemed to be always featured on "Match of the Day" then, but they were brilliant to watch and they became everyone's second team. They even beat us once 10-4, so I always hated it when we played them in London.

At this time, they had in their ranks ex-Liverpool goalie, and England stalwart Ray Clemence, and at centre-half a young Richard Gough. Years later he signed for the Blues (I think he was 72 at the time) but he was brilliant for us, which made you realise what a good player he was when he was young. They also had two England stars and media darlings in Glen Hoddle and Chris Waddle, two very skilful players, and if you add that to the predator goal scoring skills of Clive Allen, they were formidable opposition. I think our injury situation caught up with us, and we were easily beaten 2-0, with Allen netting both.

The next game deserves to be glossed over as three days later, we were thrashed 4-1 at home by Liverpool, in a bizarre cup called Screen Sport Super Cup, which was probably only ever played once, and I think over two legs. I was surprised both teams put out their 1st teams, but Everton's had been severely weakened, and although it is no fun to be beaten so heavily by your rivals, I don't think Evertonians took it very seriously. If we had won we would have done.

It was reported that instead of giving the team the usual day off after a match, Kendall had all the team in the next day to watch a video of the match. He called it a Hammer Horror.

It was rumoured that Howard liked his team to socialise together as a sort of bonding exercise, and one of the nights out they enjoyed was going to a Chinese or Italian restaurant. At one such restaurant, they ordered a lamb dish, and were surprised when the waiter told them it would cost £20 each. When they showed their surprise at the cost, the waiter said "It is English lamb", to which one of the players replied: "We want to eat it, not talk to it!"

****

"You were going to tell me about some of your other favourite players..."

Well, every now and again a player will emerge with the ability and personality to dominate a game, and there are not many who could do this. There were great players, but not that many who could totally influence the whole game. The great Alfredo di Stefano of Real Madrid was one, and of course George Best, and Pele. I can remember a player called Johnny Haynes, captain of Fulham and England, and he was one who could spray passes 40 yards with breathtaking accuracy and take over the game almost single-handedly.

Well we signed such a player from Celtic by the name of Bobby Collins, and when I first saw him, I thought he was the mascot. He was only 5ft 4", but what a player (someone said one of the fans tried to pick-pocket him, but I don't think anyone could stoop that low). He could not really dribble as such, but he used to dominate the whole team, with a fantastic will-to-win, superb passing ability, and strong leadership. Other players would let him have the ball as his vision for a through ball or astute switch of play was second to none, and he also weighed in with a good goal return. Nobody messed around with him, as he was a terrier in the tackle and god help anybody that 'did' him. A journalist once described him as the Jimmy Cagney of football, and this was a perfect description.

I saw him once against Liverpool at Anfield, when we won 2-0 and he just ran the whole game - it was wonderful to watch. If ever there was an example of how to have a winning attitude in any sport, it was the "Wee" man, as he was known.

"What happened to him?"

Well we signed him at the end of the Fifties, when he had already been at Celtic for about 10 years, and although I would say he turned our fortunes around within three seasons, a change of manager (Carey to Catterick) always brings a change of ideas, and he moved on to Leeds United. What a mistake by the Blues!

He went on to transform Leeds and help build the foundations of their most successful period under Don Revie, even going on to win The Footballer of the Year award. The Leeds team proved to be very competitive, hard to beat, but with a lot of skill, and I think they got it all from Collins, who today is considered a legend in the town. He also revived a few smaller teams in his veteran years, despite a horrific injury, and went on to play until he was 40. I was devastated when he left, and in my humble opinion was one of the best players Everton have ever had.

"Pops, are you crying?"

Above - Kevin Sheedy
Below - Gary Lineker and Howard Kendal

"These are photos taken at the Family Club Members day, where you could attend Bellfield for a day, usually on a pre-season Sunday, and meet the players and watch them train. No matter what the weather the players and management signed autographs and talked to the fans, and were very affable.

"I only encountered one who was in a bad mood; he was not happy when I asked him for an autograph whilst he was in the middle of lifting a heavy dumbbell in the gym. It was my fault, but when I joked I would hold the weight with one hand whilst he signed the autograph, he was not amused. I could not blame him as I did not realise he was in the middle of a serious training session."

Above - Author's son, Paul, with Alan Harper
Below - Author's son with Colin Harvey

Above - Paul Bracewell
Below - Gary Lineker

OCTOBER

At the start of the month we were gunned down for our third successive defeat by an Arsenal team, which featured a young Tony Adams, who led a defensively minded lot , who seemed to be happy to shout for offside at every opportunity. I think their back four used to practise putting the arms up in unison to influence the officials. It was said at the time that if they went one nil up, that was what it stayed at, and so it proved in this game. Their supporters usually sang " one nil to the Arsenal," repetitively. Apparently the words were relatively easy to memorise, even for the Arsenal fans.

No single individual hit the heights in this game, but Trevor Steven ran his usual marathon, Sheedy and Sharp tried to assert class, and Paul Wilkinson went close with a couple of headers. Wilkinson was a 6ft striker who made a name for himself with Grimsby, before signing for Everton in 1984-5 season. He was mainly used as an understudy to Sharp, but was getting more games in this particular season because of injuries. He was a never-say-die battler, who was good in the air and always gave 100% effort.

A week later , newly promoted Charlton Athletic beat us 3-2, despite two marvellous goals from Sheedy. Our third successive defeat against a London side. It was now looking like our bubble had burst, and we were on the slide.

"How much were the programmes then, Pops?"

60p Sunbeam, How could you ask that now when we are on the slide?

"Just curious, that's all. I suppose for a fiver then, you could go to the corner shop, and come back with a loaf of bread, a dozen eggs, a packet of fags, some chocolate bars, a few cans of beer, and a pound of cheese."

Yes, you are right, but you couldn't do that these days. Too many bloomin' security cameras.

"Many a true word is spoken in vest. Pops, sometimes you are nearly funny."

Our run of failure came to a timely end at the Dell, where we beat Southampton 2-0, with two late goals from a Trevor Steven penalty, and a Paul Wilkinson strike. We were well below strength but showed a mental and physical toughness, which enabled us to still be challenging at the top.

In the last league game of the month, we returned home to defeat Watford 3-2. It was a wind swept game, and we had to come from behind to win. The conditions were that bad that Trevor Steven tried several attempts to anchor the ball to take a penalty. Just as he did so, a photographer's groundsheet floated across the goal, and the referee ordered a re-take. The ice cool Steven, made an even more impressive job of his second shot.

Hero of the hour was Derek Mountfield with two goals, although he also scored an own goal. Worth noting, is that Watford gained a penalty when a certain John Barnes, who found fame as manager of Tranmere Rovers, was brought down.

Watford fans were very loud in the first half, but at half time I think they put some motor oil in their pies.

"Why?"

Not a squeak out of them in the second half.

In midweek, to finish the month, we defeated Sheffield Wed.4-0 at home in the Littlewoods Cup, with Paul Wilkinson notching 2 goals. It was hardly a surprise as Wed had not beaten us in any game since 1965 and not since 1954 in Cup football.

****

Notes of interest this month

Kevin Sheedy was selected by Jack Charlton for Ireland versus Scotland, for whom Graeme Sharp was playing on his 26th Birthday.

A centre forward was being interviewed on T.V., and remarked that:- "It is far better to go around a defender than through him" and "You cannot score if you don't shoot" Believe it or not, these were described as the best tips he had ever received. Makes you wonder what the worst tips were.

The average age of Everton's first team squad was approximately 25.

****

"Tell me more about your favourite players when you were young".

Well, no Evertonian who saw them will forget "The Holy Trinity", our dynamic midfield trio of Kendall, Ball, and Harvey. They all had skill, passion, mobility, will-to-win, and great football brains. Alan Ball was probably the most famous because he had starred for England in the 66 World Cup, and you could say he was the crowd pleaser as he seemed to cover every inch of ground.

I remember at the start of the 1969/70 season, we came out with an new look of white socks, and the football we played was absolutely brilliant.

The ball just seemed to be zipping from one set of white socks to another, and you just knew we had a great team, and so it proved when we went on to win the League title.

Howard went on to manage us in our most successful era, ably assisted by Colin Harvey, but Alan Ball, like Bobby Collins, left the club far too early, to Arsenal, and went on to great things. Another mistake on our part, but who knows what goes on behind the scenes.

NOVEMBER

"What was it like going to the match in those days?"

It was really exciting, because we were always confident we were going to win. We normally played a 4-4-2 system, and used to dominate games, with it being only a matter of time before we scored.

The defence was well organised with strong athletic players who were very quick. In the centre of midfield we possessed very hard workers, who were terriers in the tackle. On the flanks we had two skilful men who could deliver good crosses and also score goals. Up front we always played two strikers, who never gave defenders time on the ball, and they were also good at taking chances.

Probably the best team in the world at the time were AC Milan, and the feature of their game was when they lost the ball, they closed their opponents down very quickly and hunted them down until they got it back, and then the skill and flair took over. Everton were the same, but on a smaller stage.

"Did the crowd have favourites?"

I think individually you did, but I think it was a measure of a good team, that I think everyone was liked. I cannot remember any player ever being picked on.

The principle of our football was that when we lost the ball, we chased and harried the opposition very quickly, and when we were in possession, we passed it well and attacked. I think the ball players were encouraged to show their tricks but only in the right areas. If you add a fine team spirit aided by a positive mentality, it produces a winning formula, which was very enjoyable to watch.

"What did you do on match days?"

I used to take your aunty and uncle at that time. She was 10 and he was 14, and we would go in the Blues Family Club, which was situated in the Upper Bullens Road Stand. The club was a fairly new idea and they moved it around a bit in the early years, before they settled in lower Goodison Road. It would cost me £5.20, and £ 2.30 per child. Add to that a few packets of crisps, a lemonade, some chocolate bars, and it was a good value for money day out. I cannot remember what the children ate.

Our first game in November was away to West Ham Utd., and it just shows you how much we had progressed because we were quoted at being dumfounded to lose 1-0, after dominating play. We completely outplayed the Hammers, but could not burst their bubbles. Included in their team were two future Evertonians, Mark Ward and Tony Cottee. The only goal was a rare header from Alan Dickens, their midfielder being hailed as the new Trevor Brooking, the West Ham legend.

The lads returned to Goodison the following week to a fiery clash with Chelsea. This seemed to be the norm in those days, when the Londoners were not the force they are now with " loads of money". The tricky Scots winger Pat Nevin was a Chelsea star, who later signed for us. Despite Chelsea only having 10 men, they forced us to a 2-2 draw, with Sheedy and Steven (pen) our scorers. Sheedy`s goal was particularly clever, as it was struck from 12 yards (free-kick) with a ten man defensive wall blocking the whole goal line. These kicks are very rarely converted.

A comfortable away win at Leicester got us back to winning ways. Scorers were Heath and Sheedy, but our "man of the match" was goalie Neville Southall. It was reported that his handling was never less than sound. He showed great courage coming off his line fast whenever required, and to cap it all he produced four magnificent saves that ultimately proved the difference between defeat and victory. It just shows you how important in the long run a good quality goalkeeper is, and often proves he is responsible for winning the points.

For the first half of the season, Big Nev, as he was affectionately known, had been injured and Bobby Mimms had deputised. Mimms was a tall, very competent keeper, who would have commanded a first team place anywhere, but at Everton, he was always going to be an understudy. The reason was Southall was probably the best goalie in the world at the time. He had every physical attribute needed and was a very strong character.

In midweek we beat Norwich away in the League Cup 4th Round. Scorers were Steven, Heath, Sharp, and Sheedy. A good win but the fans were more interested in the League, and were looking forward to a serious derby match at home on the following Saturday.

After a lengthy period of derby matches in which goals flowed and good football was mixed with power, passion and humour, this match, a 0-0 draw was a big let down for the best crowd of the season - 48,000 - and the nationwide TV audience.

The large crowd normally so receptive to the atmosphere of these meetings, greeted the final whistle with a few jeers and then silence. They had expected something better. It was no surprise that Everton's M.O.M. was defender Kevin Ratcliffe, and Liverpool's was Mark Lawrenson, who went on to find fame as a TV pundit..

Kevin Ratcliffe was our captain, and commanded a lot of respect. He came up through our youth system and started as a left fullback before moving into the centre of defence. He read the game well, and was a strong tackler, but probably his greatest strength was his pace and speed of recovery. A player that was very hard to play against.

Full teams for the derby:-

Everton: Southall: Harper, Power, Ratcliffe, Mountfield: Langley (Wilkinson 74), Steven, Heath, Sharp, Adams, Sheedy.

Liverpool: Grobbelaar: Gillespie, Beglin, Lawrenson, Whelan,

Hansen, Walsh, Nicol, Rush, Molby, McMahon.

(Luckily many of these Liverpool players went on to forge better careers for themselves and found fame in other areas of the game).

At this point Arsenal were top, Liverpool were 3rd and Everton 4th.

We returned to winning ways with a comfortable 3-1 away win at Man. City, who had sunk to the bottom of the league. This was our first win at Maine Road since 1972. Heath notched 2, and Paul Power scored against his old team, but refused to celebrate. Kendall and Power both uttered the time honoured "kiss of death" phrase - "City are too good to go down".

Paul Power was a stalwart at Man.City and had spent 11 seasons with them, when Kendall surprisingly signed him prior to the start of the season. Although he was considered a veteran at 33, he was very fit with a reputation for being a good professional. Like Ratters he was a natural left footer and he slotted in well at left back, and was renowned for "bombing" down the line to support the attack. His signing was later described as "the signing of the season" in many quarters, especially with Mrs. Power.

DECEMBER

First game of the month - Full Members Cup versus Newcastle.

"What was that all about? Pops"

I think it was introduced because all our teams had been banned from Europe because of hooliganism. Did you know that at that time, the papers found that one fan was getting mugged at every match, and I tell you what he was getting bloomin annoyed about it.

Our supporters voted with their feet as only 7,000 turned up to see us thrash Newcastle 5-2. What was surprising is that we fielded the 1ˢᵗ team. Probably a condition of the cup rules.

A powerful display with goals from Power, Pointon, Steven, and Heath secured a 4-0 win at home to Norwich. A fixture which had an inevitably about it.

Graeme Sharp was given a holiday break over Xmas, when he was booked for the sixth time this season in the 1-0 defeat at Luton. This was our first reverse in 8 matches. Was it something to do with the plastic pitch, since banned, and the fact Luton had banned all away supporters. What a farce!

Although Arsenal were top, manager George Graham predicted Everton to win the league, and also the Bookies made us favourites, even though we were 4 points behind the Gunners.

Christmas was coming and our stockings were being filled with points. Dave Bassett, manager of Wimbledon admitted Everton's 3-0 win at Goodison was a triumph of football over booting.

Using a Christmas analogy, he remarked "it was our first stuffing of the season". Watching Wimbledon play football was like watching rawboned Marines racing around an assault course. Their idea of football was to get the ball into the last third of the pitch by kicking it high and long, and hoping one of their players gets on the end of it. Everton got there by a series of accurate passes, and class told in this game, with goals from Steven, Sheedy, and Heath.

I loved it when we played at home on Boxing Day - used to make Christmas - always a big crowd and great atmosphere, but this time we were away at Newcastle. This game we were right on form and destroyed them, putting them deep into relegation trouble. Star of the show was Geordie boy, "Tricky" Trevor Steven, with 2 goals, and a display rich in skill and artistry. Heath and Power got the other goals in a 4-0 win.

Steven was signed from Burnley a few years earlier. He played there as a midfielder, but Kendall turned him into an international right winger. He possessed a lot of skill, which earned him the nickname of "Tricky", as he could beat a man, but also a hard worker down the right flank. Only 5ft 8in, but a wonderful team player and great to watch.

Kendall praised his men" You've done me proud. That was something rather special, but I also want the players to know that I won't be happy until we are top of the league with points in hand." Howard never settled for second best.

Two days later, we returned to Goodison to put on another great display of power, hammering Leicester City 5-1. It was reported that Everton's mean machine bid fond farewell to 1986 in glorious style. What a Christmas for all Blues fans. They picked up where they left off at St. James` Park, mercilessly punishing the slightest of errors and producing the sort of clinical finishing which not only win games but trophies. We were in breathtaking form against a mediocre team, in what should have been a cricket score. Heath and Wilkinson with 2 a-piece, plus a classic cheeky lob from Sheedy got the goals. Nearly 40,000 went home happy.

The author, son Paul and daughter Jennie with the Football League Championship trophy and the Charity Shield. In the background, suitably, are the Liverpudlians: daughter Naomi and wife Paula.

JANUARY

It was always an exciting holiday atmosphere to attend a game on New Year's day. Everybody seemed in a good mood, with the joys of the night before being carried over. It was even better when your team had just won three in a row and were second in the league, and were about to take on opponents who were second from bottom.

For some reason, I only paid £4.70 for the Family Club - perhaps because it was in the Lower Bullens Road stand and not the Upper - to watch us struggle in the first half against a weak Aston Villa side, but improved in the second to run out as comfortable 3-0 winners. Before a healthy crowd of 40,000 plus, goals by Harper, Steven, and Sheedy (him again) ensured victory.

Two items of note, was that Villa were managed by former Celtic stalwart Billy McNeil, who observed that "Everton were a good side, who could go on to win the Championship." Andy Gray, our ex-hero, returned to Goodison for the first time since his transfer, and was given a rapturous welcome by the crowd, but he made no impression on the game. Aston Vanilla - we licked them!

Two days later we had to play QPR away, on their plastic pitch. Everton had not won in 6 attempts on artificial surfaces, and manager Howard Kendall announced we would be modifying our game plan to suit the conditions. Whether it was a touch of psychology I don't know, but he said they had a "secret plan".

Graeme Sharp returned to the attack from suspension, with perfect timing as he got the only goal of the game. Despite the result, Kendall said he still hated plastic pitches.

It was reported that Spanish agents were watching Michael Robinson who was playing for QPR. This was surprising because he was a bustling all action type of forward, not what you think would suit

Spanish football, but he eventually ended up there, via Liverpool, and carved out a fine career for himself, and is now very famous as a commentator there.

****

The big news on the transfer front was that Everton had won the great Mersey tug-of-war to sign the precocious talent of Ian Snodin from Leeds Utd. The reported news was that both Everton and Liverpool had offered the same fee of £840,000 for the 23 year old, but he decided to join us. His decision was regarded as a major turning point in the history of the two clubs. By rejecting a move to Anfield, and Britain's most successful club, he had finally buried the myth that Liverpool simply had to show interest to automatically guarantee they got their man.

The fans were chuffed about this, but he was only an England under 21 international so as far as I was concerned he had a lot to prove. His reasons for joining us were; "Everton have a lot of good young players and I see them at the top of the ladder for the next three or four years". All the usual clichés were bandied about from the Blues, "delighted to get him", "huge potential", blah, blah. Kendall summed it up by stating "we are only winners if he does it on the field". He was a combative mid-field player with skill, and most fans were excited by the capture.

The timing of the signing was probably hastened by the news that the long term future of mid-fielder Paul Bracewell was a worry. He was to have more surgery on his damaged ankle, and having not played all season, his future did not look bright.

****

First week in a cold and wet January, is traditionally 3rd round of the FA cup, and it resulted in a comfortable 2-1 home win against Southampton., who had Mark Wright in their line-up, later to play for

Liverpool and find fame was Manager of Chester City. One of their subs, was a young Matt Le Tissier. Two goals for Sharpy clinched victory.

Ian Snodin made his debut as a sub against mid table Sheffield Wed. who had his brother Glyn at left back, together with ex Blues Martin Hodge and Gary Megson.

Goals from Trevor Steven (pen) and Dave Watson, ensured the win, which was marred by an injury picked up by Dave Watson, which would rule him out for the forthcoming Derby match in the next round of the Littlewoods Cup.

The mid -week derby was a typical pulsating affair, marred by a tragic injury to the Liverpool left back, Jim Beglin, who suffered a broken leg. The only goal of the game came from Ian Rush, 6 minutes from time, which sent Kenny's men into their 7th semi-final in 8 years. Rush's goal was his 17th in 19 clashes against us, only 2 behind the record set by Dixie Dean. Rush was bound for Juventus at the end of the season, and we would be glad to see the back of him.

A newspaper assessment of the Toffees at this stage stated they had gone back to their old pattern of playing as a team, whereas last year they tended to depend on Gary Lineker, and play to his strengths. By January, they had managed to sustain their First Division strength in the absence, through injury, of international stars.

With these absentees about to return, the signs were ominous for their rivals. The Press were forecasting second place, with Arsenal as champions.

A second successive defeat against arch rivals Notts Forest (1-0) set back the Blues, but it was generally felt we had dominated the game and created many chances against a team who were unbeaten at home. It was Ian Snodin's full debut..

Towards the end of the month, we suffered another injury setback when Kevin Sheedy was ruled out for 6 weeks. Top scorer Sheedy had a cartilage operation barely an hour after visiting a specialist for a check on his troublesome knee.

It is worth pointing out that in those days, we had a proper reserve league, called the Central League, which was very competitive, with first team players playing regularly there if they were dropped or returning from injury. We even had a third team, called the 'A' team, and many stars started the road to recovery in this team. Everton had a talented backroom staff in Coaches Mick Heaton, Colin Harvey, Terry Darracott (ex-player) and Youth team coach, Graham Smith. Not as big an entourage as they have now, but probably more effective.

Derek Mountfield, who had been replaced at the centre of defence by Dave Watson, had a transfer request turned down, as Kendall wanted to maintain the strength in depth of the squad.

The next game was the 4th round of the FA Cup at Bradford, and Peter Reid and Pat Van den Hauwe were recalled. Reid had only played just one game this season, and Pat was playing in his first as he had been out with a blood disorder followed by a muscle strain.

Both put on 5 star displays, but our MOM was Ian Snodin, who scored the only goal of the game with his first ever headed goal. Snodin was anxious to please in front of a Valley Parade crowd who had not forgotten his Leeds Utd connections, and booed him whenever he touched the ball.

Star man for Bradford was midfielder Stuart McCall, a future Blue.

FEBRUARY

The month began with a home game against Coventry City, who were mid-table. It was a notable occasion as it was 30 year old Peter Reid's first home game in 8 months, following a stress fracture of the ankle. Reid was a Huyton lad who had been signed from Bolton a few seasons ago. He had a history of injuries, but we took a chance and were well rewarded, as he was an inspirational player with a never-say-die attitude, and could see a good pass. He gained England recognition, and if you look back on old TV clips, you will see him trying to catch Maradona scoring a fabulous goal against England. He had more chance of catching the wind.

Pat van Den Hauwe also made his first home appearance. These were two major players from the previous two years so it was massive boost. A good 3-1 win saw us go top of the table for the first time this season, just above Arsenal and Liverpool.

I don't know what Bill Shanks would have said.

On to the university city of Oxford to play Utd, where at the end of a bad tempered affair, Howard had to guide his players away from the trouble at the end of the game. They were described as ugly scenes, but Big Nev typically remarked, "It's a man's game"

Paul Wilkinson took the place of the injured Graeme Sharp, and he hooked in for the equaliser with 2 minutes to go.

We were steamrolled out of the FA Cup 5th round by Wimbledon in a televised match. "We were out-powered and out gunned" remarked Howard, "and now we can concentrate on the league". This was an old cliché, but never had it been truer.

The fans were generally disappointed as it robbed us of potentially a record fourth successive Wembley appearance - we were just getting greedy.

Many teams were being steamrolled by Wimbledon at this time, and they were not popular with the football public.

A sunny day in Manchester resulted in a 0-0 draw in a hard, bruising, unrelenting battle at Old Trafford. This point was not enough to prevent Liverpool taking over at the top of the league.

Entertainment value was described as nil, in an untidy war of attrition with bumps, bruises, and physical encounters a regular occurrence. Utd had had a poor season and were in the bottom half of the league, and were fighting for their pride as it had been almost 5 years since they last beat Everton in the league.

****

Howard Kendall again proved his astuteness in the transfer market with the signing of striker Wayne Clarke, whose subsequent goals were a godsend. It was reported that Everton had paid Birmingham City £300,000 for Clarke and a young winger named Stuart Storer, who was really only a makeweight in the deal, as Clarke was valued at £250,000, but Birmingham were to receive only £165,000 of the deal, as there was a sell-on clause in the players transfer from Wolves three years earlier.

Clarke was the younger brother of Alan, who had been a very successful striker for Leeds and England, and was now manager of Barnsley. He had the same style as his older brother, but lacked his aggression and speed, but he had a good scoring record at Brum (19 goals this season) so was well worth a punt. Sharp had been injured and Paul Wilkinson, although a trier, was not scoring the goals.

Along with Snodin, this proved a significant capture in the long run.

"Pops, if you had one chance to see again just one player at his peak, who would it be?"

That is easy.

There have been great players who could run all day, tackle, head, score goals, and be what most managers want , particularly today, and that is all round athletes. But I am a great believer in that football is an entertainment and you want to witness someone doing what an ordinary player could not do.

This player had a style that was unique, and did things that took your breath away.

He had something called charisma.

"What's that?"

It is something I possess.

"I thought that was arthritis."

When this 'vision' ran, he seemed to glide over the ground. He shimmied, and flicked, back-heeled, waltzed past players, scored goals. You just could not wait for the ball to go to him to see what he would do.

I once saw him chasing a ball to the side line towards the Paddock, with a defender in hot pursuit just behind him. He really had nowhere to go, but he stopped the ball and turned and pushed the ball through the opponents legs and was away. It seemed to happen all in one graceful moment. The crowd just seemed to gasp for breath, before breaking into rapturous applause.

Another time, I remember the ball going over the centre-half's head, Bill Foulkes of Man.Utd, towards the far post, when he leaped, like a salmon, and headed back towards the same way the ball had come, and curved it right into the top corner of the net.

Everything he did, he did with such grace and elegance. I would pay to just go and watch him. The best footballer Everton have ever had.

"What was his name?"

For the life of me, I cannot remember.

"You're teasing me now. Was it Alex Young?"

Of course.

"Well, what made him different say from the other greats?"

He was probably not as hard-working, could not tackle, and was a bit inconsistent, but he was an artist. If you asked any Blue that if he could witness 90 minutes of a player playing at his absolute peak, in prime condition, it would be Alex.

He was magic, and if ever a player deserved his nickname, it was him - 'The Golden Vision'.

"I take it you liked him, Pops".

The author, son Paul and daughter Jennie with the Cannon League Championship trophy, the European Cup Winners Cup, and the Charity Shield.

MARCH

"Pops, I noticed we lost to Watford at the start of the month. Were they any good ?"

Yes, they were at the time. We had beaten them in the FA Cup Final a few years earlier, and they were now an established First Division team.

"Who were their stars?"

Probably Elton John, who was their Chairman.

Well, did you notice how short the shorts were then. A very young John Barnes, who starred on the wing for them and later found fame as manager of Tranmere, was said to have the biggest thighs in football.

"How come the shorts were so short? They would be arrested now."

I think it was because they were athletes, it was thought they would give them more freedom of movement. In theory I suppose you could run faster with more freedom of movement.

Not a good start to the month, a 2-1 defeat. Heath getting our goal, and to make matters worse, our ex-player, Kevin Richardson starred for them. The swinehund!!

Wayne Clarke made an encouraging debut, and the papers stated he looked like becoming a useful acquisition.

****

Southampton were our next visitors, and they were in need of precious points. Matthew Le Tissier was their up and coming shining light and had grabbed a hat-trick in his previous game, and this was his first season in the first team, having scored 56 times in reserve football last season.

Although he was a wonderful ball player, he never got a look-in against our disciplined teamwork.

Our 3-0 win kept us in hot pursuit of league leaders Liverpool.

I asked a 'Red' what he thought of the situation, and he replied "I don't know what Shankly would have said".

A poor crowd of 26,000, probably because it was cold and drizzly, saw an OG by Mark Wright, a Paul Power effort and a rare one from Watson sealing the win.

At this stage the title looked like it was between us, Liverpool, and Arsenal, whose manager George Graham maintained his squad were not strong enough for a title challenge. You would probably not believe it but in 4th and 5th spot respectively were Luton Town and Norwich City.

Our next home game was against lowly Charlton, who unbelievably had beaten us twice earlier in the season: 3-2 at Selhurst Park (their temporary ground as their new stadium was being built) in the league, and in some 'Mickey Mouse' cup competition.

This was the type of the game you went to expecting an easy victory, but we only managed a 2-1 win, with Snodin and a Charlton player sent off for a flare-up. Heath scored our first, and Gary Stevens scored the winner with a rare late strike.

After this game we were 6 points behind Kenny Dalglish's Liverpool with 2 games in hand. At this stage the Reds were quoted at 4-7 for the title and we were 2-1. I don't know what Shankly would have said.

Adrian Heath, known as "Inchy" because he was only about 5ft 6 ins tall, had had a great season.

He had been in the doldrums for the past 2 years playing second fiddle to Andy Gray and Gary Lineker, but this season he had played in midfield and up front alongside Graeme Sharp. A very skilful player, always busy, and a natural goalscorer. If I was going to nominate a favourite player, he would be on my 'Short' list.

Gary Stevens worked his way through to the first team from joining as an apprentice. Very fit and athletic. Wingers found him very hard to beat, and his consistent displays earned him many caps for England. He had a close partnership down the right flank with Trevor Steven.

****

Transfer news

Paul Wilkinson decided to move to Brian Clough's Notts Forest. Probably it was the signing of Wayne Clarke that helped make the decision, but he had never really established himself at Everton.

With Sheedy and Sharp due to return to action, the Blues sat through the transfer deadline day without adding to the squad.

****

We were getting to the 'business' end of the season now, and we faced two daunting away fixtures in London, first at Arsenal and then Chelsea.

This was an Arsenal side containing the likes of O'Leary, Adams, Quinn, and Nicholas, so no easy task. The home side had set the pace earlier in the season, but they had been faltering of late, with rumours that they had been fielding weakened teams as they wanted to concentrate on their forthcoming Littlewoods Cup final versus Liverpool.

A blunder by goalkeeper John Lukic in the 21st minute allowed a supreme piece of opportunism by Wayne Clarke to snatch the only goal of the game. It was reported that Everton played like a team possessed, with Snodin and Reid running themselves into the ground, but our MOM was Neville Southall, who proved an impenetrable barrier pulling off many fine saves.

After this victory we were 3 points behind Liverpool with 2 games in hand, Liverpool having lost at home to Wimbledon in what looked like a home banker. I don't know what you know who would have said!

****

"What were the crowds like in those days?"

Funnily enough, not as big as today. Man.U had the biggest average - about 38,000 - followed by Liverpool with 36,000 and then us on 32,000. Chelsea's average was only 16,000. But we were better looking than today's lot.

"Did you still have perms and shell suits?"

No, only Humpty Dumpty was still wearing his shell suit, and he was due a big fall.

We had our own Fan Club at Everton. It cost £10 per year and you received 12 monthly mags, a membership diploma signed by Howard Kendall and Kevin Ratcliffe, plus a souvenir bronze medallion wall plaque with engraved autographs of the first team squad.

"I'm impressed, I'm impressed !"

It was described as the hotline to the dressing room. You could also buy video tapes of every home game, price £13.99, so not cheap. We also had a famous mascot, called the Toffee lady, who used to dress in an outfit similar to a traditional Welsh national dress, only in blue. She used to walk around the ground before kick-off throwing toffees into the crowd. I think this tradition was stopped because of Health and Safety reasons - probably they got scared in case somebody claimed one of the sweets had hit them in the eye, causing them to stay off work for 6 months.

"Have you any more information that I can bore my mates with at school?"

How about this? Our away strip was yellow, the kit was made by Umbro, the ball by Mitre, and the tea served by Nellie and Norah.
Bells Whisky sponsored Manager of the Month/Year and Kendall won it that often he could have started an Off-License
We were sponsored by the NEC Corporation, a company who made computers and we wore the NEC logo on our shirts.

Our highest attendance was 48,247 against Liverpool - our capacity has since been reduced following the implementation of all seater stadiums.

Anything else you would like to know ?

"No, I am going home now for a lie down - in a darkened room."

I'll get your anorak.

APRIL

Our second trip to London on the first week of April produced another fine victory 2-1 against Chelsea, with goals from Watson and Harper, who thundered in a 30 yard wonder goal. This was Peter Reid's seventh game back, and in it he produced his best form.

"Pops, why were Chelski just an ordinary team then?"

They did not have a mega rich owner who could buy any of the top players from around the world. Most teams were made up of players from the British Isles, who had come through the Juniors, and when a team signed anyone, it was usually from Scotland, where there seemed a rich vein of talent. I think even the Krankies would have got a game at some of the teams.

"Who ran the clubs then?"

Well clubs had a board of directors, headed by a chairman, and these guys were usually well-off business men, to whom football was a hobby. They no doubt dug deep into their own pockets to finance the club, but not to present day scale. Most clubs were owned by shareholders, who were mainly fans. The Chairman of Everton was Sir Philip Carter, who left for a while, but has since returned. The secretary was Jim Greenwood.

It was rumoured that a lot of clubs were experiencing financial difficulties, and were in danger of winding up, but most have survived to continue the struggle.

****

Having seen off Arsenal and Chelsea, on their way back to the top, a very confident Blues blasted West Ham to complete a cockney treble. Clarke, Reid, Stevens, and Watson got all 4 goals in a dynamic first half.

After the game Howard stated "our first half performance was as a pleasing 45 minutes as I have seen all season."
He warned fans against over confidence as Liverpool had been beaten at Norwich (Oh, dear, what would have Shanks said?).

There was a report that Paul Bracewell had had his plaster removed from his ankle following his fourth operation, and that ex-team-mate Gary Lineker had invited him to stay for a week at his Barcelona home. Bracewell said "It is a great gesture and I appreciate it. Gary has a pool and a gym (ooooh!) so I can do some work. But I will be on crutches another two weeks and then it's a matter of almost complete rest until the start of pre-season training".

I wrote to Gary and told him to put me down for the last week in July and first week in August, but I got no reply.

Spurs were making a late dash clearing up a backlog of fixtures, but the title looked like a two horse race between the Merseyside giants, but with a little blue gap opening up.

There was good news for fans mid-week as three established star performers came through a reserve game to set themselves up for selection. Graeme Sharp, who had been a non-starter in 13 of the last 14 games, Pat Van Den Hauwe (the popular Welsh cheeky chappie) and Ian Snodin (available after suspension).

Aston Villa at Villa Park is traditionally a daunting away fixture, but at this point Villa were second from bottom with relegation looking certain. Former Blues players Keown and Gray were in their line-up, but they were no threat, and Southall was not seriously troubled. Everton never really reached the heights, but a solitary goal by Sheedy was enough to keep the crucial 3 points ahead of Liverpool. Shanks would have been speechless.

The next visitors to Goodison were a lowly Newcastle, and Wayne Clarke's first ever league hat-trick secured our seventh successive win, even without the injured Sheedy and Reid. Utility player Alan Harper again emphasised his invaluable worth. The Magpies had a young Gascoigne in midfield, and he managed to get himself booked. At full-back, they had another future Blue in Neil McDonald, who was sent off in the last minute. An excellent crowd of 44,000 witnessed the easy victory.

The last game of the month was the clash of the giants at Anfield, and a 3-1 victory by the Reds ensured the title race was still bubbling over into May, with the Blues still favourites. The Derby was described as a classic, but it was really a huge disappointment to Evertonians, as their jinx, Ian Rush, scored 2 goals. Apparently this pleased a Juventus delegation in the stands, who could not wait to take him to Turin. As far as we were concerned he should have gone to Italy straight from Chester City.

The papers reported there was fierce but fair tackling in midfield between Reid and Steve McMahon (ex blue) and the supporters showed their mutual respect.

I don't know what Harry Catterick would have said.

There was a terrible storm that night, and it was said four Liverpudlians were killed by a fallen tree.

"You are joking, Pops?"

A spokesman for the police said " we did not even know they were living up there"

MAY

The next home game, against bottom of the league Man.City, was down as a banker, but whether it was the importance of the occasion, it fizzled out into a surprise 0-0 draw. To add more misery, Clarke dislocated a shoulder in a late collision with City keeper Eric Nixon (future Tranmere favourite) and was ruled out for the last 3 games. MOM was Mick McCarthy, the City centre half, now manager of Wolves.

Crunch time came with an away fixture at Norwich City - 3 points and the title would be ours. 7000 fans made the round trip to see a thoroughly professional performance gain the win and hence the championship. The unlikely goalscorer was tough-tackling full-back Pat Van den Hauwe, after only 45 seconds, driving the ball into the top of the net from close in. Norwich were a hard side to beat at home, but once we took the lead, we tightened the grip on the game, built on solid defence held together by Dave Watson, who 12 months earlier had captained Norwich to the Second Division title.

There were wild celebrations at the end of the match, with skipper Kevin Ratcliffe being carried round the field.

Five days later 44,000 fans packed Goodison Park to celebrate the title in a carnival atmosphere. It started with a ticker-tape welcome and ended with the championship trophy being presented to captain Kevin Ratcliffe, amid hysterical scenes. In-between was an entertaining encounter with a competitive performance from Luton Town, which the Blues won 3-1. Everton's manager Howard Kendall said "It was a marvellous occasion and a wonderful night. I'm just proud to be a part of it."

Luton made things hot for the Blues by taking the lead through Mark Stein. Peter Reid's shot rebounded from the bar, but the hawk-eyed referee spotted that a Luton defender had handled, and Steven slotted home the pen. Only a few moments later Steven earned a second pen. when he was shoved off the ball, and he duly converted again. The final goal was a deflection from Sharp.

The one last re-arranged game versus Spurs was a bit of a non- event, with Derek Mountfield clinching a 1-0 victory on a Monday evening. Spurs were due to play in the FA Cup final on the following Saturday, and so fielded virtually a reserve team, resulting in an FA enquiry and a possible fine. Their defiant manager, David Pleat, insisted "our first team would have been beaten by more."

****

To sum up...

Kevin Ratcliffe was the only ever-present, playing 42 games (there were 22 teams in the League then). Heath and Steven made 41 appearances. And Power 40.

Leading league goal scorer was Trevor Steven with 14, followed by Sheedy with 13 and Heath with 11.

As points of interest, Leicester City, Man. City, and Aston Villa were relegated. Coventry surprised everybody by beating Spurs in the FA Cup final.

Quotes:

"Even when we were nine points adrift, we always felt we would come back to win" - Kevin Ratcliffe.

"I'd have to say this was an even greater achievement than the last one" - Howard Kendall.

"The pies are sound, La." - Fat Joe in the Gladwys St.

CONCLUSION

A terrible injury list at the start of the season, but we managed to hold on with some good results, and the experience we had gained over the previous two seasons had stood us in good stead. The manager made excellent signings in Watson, Snodin, Power and Clarke, and when the top players started coming back from injury, it was like the cavalry arriving at the right time.

Nowadays we probably would not be able to hang on to our stars for so long, as the mega rich clubs would have snapped them up. It is all about money these days.

Probably the main reason we won the title was the fantastic management skills of Howard Kendall. Apparently he was great at communication, and being a magnificent footballer himself, he was a first class tactician and knew the game inside out. It was reported that he managed with a lot of laughter, no bull shine, and a minimum of team meetings. He seemed to have the respect of the players, and certainly the fans. Teamwork was his watchword, and this proved to be the key ingredient, as the club was dogged by one injury after another. He is arguably the best manager we had ever had, and at the end of the season, he was deservedly named Bells Manager of the Year (by the way, Harry Rednapp won the divisional award whilst at Bournemouth).

Whilst there is no doubt about Howard's management skills, I don't think his assistant, Colin Harvey, got as much credit as he deserved for his part for Everton's success during this period. He was one of the good guys, but quiet and unassuming, which is probably why he was overlooked by the media. He was eventually to succeed Howard, but that is another story.

Everton had a group of "winners" - players who hated being beaten at anything - but they also were very skilful, what a combination. Add to this a great team spirit and look out!

The League title was a culmination of a period of success, which breeds confidence, a great group of players and top management. Who was to know it was all soon to break up and leave Everton struggling for a long time. Looking back, a lot of the personnel left too soon and they were difficult to replace.

During the title run-in our nearest rivals, Liverpool, lost 4 out of the last 8 games, and we only lost one to - guess who? - Liverpool.

At the end of the day, we had won the league and beaten our near neighbours by 9 points to boot - I just don't know what Shankly would have said.

"Pops, after all you have told me...why do I stick up for Liverpool?"

ADDENDUM

These are poems I wrote during recent transfer windows.

The first one reflects the frustration of the fans who are awaiting a signing, but nothing seems to be happening, and the window is approaching closure.

Have we signed anyone yet?

I get up in the morning, the weather's still cold and wet.
I shout down to the missus,
Have we signed anyone yet?

I search through all the papers, might just have a little bet,
A cry comes from the kitchen,
Have we signed anyone yet?

I watch the latest news, the country's all in debt,
Who cares about the credit crunch?
Have we signed anyone yet?

My son , at work, has text me, his lunch he has just ate,
Hey dad, what's the latest?
Have we signed anyone yet?

I take the dog for a walk, I know I shouldn't fret,
But I rush back for the sports report,
Have we signed anyone yet?

The evening is coming on, no player's escaped our net,
I greet my mates in the pub,
Have we signed anyone yet?

The chippy is somewhat crowded, put a fish in for me, pet,
There is just one thing to ask,
Have we signed anyone yet?

I settle in my favourite chair, and switch on the TV set,
You will never guess, dear blue boys,
Still not signed anyone yet.

But tomorrow is another day, and the deadline does draw near,
I am not going to think about it anymore,
Pour myself another beer.

This is the follow-up poem, when we did eventually sign someone, but nobody had heard of him.

The signing

The white smoke is arising, the stork is on the way,
The birth of a new era, oh what a perfect day!

Gold medals are so good, this is better than that,
I'd throw it in the air, if I only owned a hat.

Raise your voices high, till your throats are sore.
We'll rock in Gladwys St., Revive the Goodison roar.

Oh what a wonderful life, oh what a happy blue
Surely finish 5th again, maybe a cup or two.

I'll not forget this moment, like a sailor going home,
A brand new transfer signing, and not even one on loan.

I almost spilt my beer, cried when I heard the news,
The missus shouted up to me, there's a new player for the blues.

But in my mind there is a doubt, a worry, I declare

I just cannot help a-wondering,
Who are yer? Who are yer?

The transfer dream

I had a dream about the transfer window, and we had zillions of dough,
Just who would we spend it on, where would the money go?

I dreamt we had signed a keeper, with hands as big as Neville's,
Just his presence in the box eliminates defensive perils.

At the back, we'd got a giant,with a heart as big as stone.
With a brain from the life of Brian, and the class of Mr. Labone.

In midfield we'd bought a dynamite, only small, but had it all.
How much would these now cost, Kendall, Harvey, and Ball.

I thought we'd sign a vision, a man with golden hair.
He could dribble, just like Alex, young with grace and flair.

I dreamt I was in heaven, it was the perfect dream,
We'd signed a centre forward, who could head like Dixie Dean.

Someone famous once had a dream, but not as good as mine,
When a dream comes true, it dies, my dream lasts for all time.

Other books by the same author
also published by Countyvise

Growing Up in Liverpool Before Beatlemania

The Clubman - Tales of an Insurance Man